ON THE BALL

Amazing sports facts from football to pickleball, baseball to golf

ALF ALDERSON

This edition published in 2025
by Dog 'n' Bone Books
an imprint of Ryland
Peters & Small Ltd
20–21 Jockey's Fields
London WC1R 4BW
and
1452 Davis Bugg Road
Warrenton, NC 27589
www.rylandpeters.com
Email: euregulations@
rylandpeters.com

First published in 2016 as
Ball Sport Trivia and in 2018
as *What a Load of Balls*

10 9 8 7 6 5 4 3 2 1

Text, design, and illustration ©
Dog 'n' Bone Books 2016, 2025
For additional picture credits,
see page 96.

The author's moral rights
have been asserted. All
rights reserved. No part of this
publication may be reproduced,
stored in a retrieval system,
or transmitted in any form
or by any means, electronic,
mechanical, photocopying,
or otherwise, without the prior
permission of the publisher.

A CIP record for this book
is available from the British
Library. US Library of Congress
CIP data has been applied for.

ISBN: 978 1 912983 87 2

Printed in China

Illustrator: Blair Frame
Editor: Marion Paull
Designer: Jerry Goldie
Desk editor: Imogen Valler-Miles
Senior designer: Paul Stradling
Art director: Sally Powell
Creative director:
Leslie Harrington
Head of production:
Patricia Harrington
Publishing manager:
Carmel Edmonds

The authorised representative
in the EEA is Authorised Rep
Compliance Ltd., Ground Floor,
71 Lower Baggot Street, Dublin,
D01 P593, Ireland
www.arccompliance.com

MIX
Paper | Supporting
responsible forestry
FSC® C008047

CONTENTS

INTRODUCTION 6

BASKETBALL 8

AMERICAN FOOTBALL 16

VOLLEYBALL 24

RUGBY 28

TEN-PIN BOWLING 36

FOOTBALL/ SOCCER 38

TENNIS 48

PADEL 56

SQUASH 60

TABLE TENNIS 62

PICKLEBALL 64

CRICKET 68

BASEBALL 76

LACROSSE 84

GOLF 86

SOFTBALL 94

ACKNOWLEDGMENTS 96

PICTURE CREDITS 96

ABOUT THE AUTHOR 96

INTRODUCTION

It's a dark, cold winter night and a group of mates are, sensibly, sitting in a warm pub and discussing sport. Apropos of nothing, someone suddenly enquires, "Why are tennis balls fuzzy? And green?"

A second voice pipes up, "Yeah, and what about rugby balls—just why *are* they oval?"*

All very sound questions, but no one has an answer to any of them.

Then it's suggested that as the only journalist among the assembled throng, I should make it my job to search out and discover these facts and more about sports balls.

Well, if you think about it, we pretty much take it for granted that a football, a cricket ball, a baseball, or any other sports ball for that matter, is the shape it is, and that's that.

Yet what the *Oxford English Dictionary* defines as a "solid or hollow spherical or egg-shaped object that is kicked, thrown, or hit in a game" can be as fundamental a part of life for some people as the change in the seasons.

When a major sporting event such as the World Cup, Super Bowl, Wimbledon, the Masters, the World Series, or the Ashes is underway, life pretty much stops for some of us as we take time off work, skip school, or stay up late to watch a ball hit the back of a net, sail between the posts, or cross a boundary.

So it seems only decent to take a moment or two to consider the history of, and reasons behind, why your favorite sport uses a round or oval ball, a small or large ball, or a heavy or light ball.

For true believers, what Liverpool FC manager Bill Shankly famously said of soccer—known to him and many others as simply football—could be applied to most ball sports: "***Some people believe football is a matter of life and death … It is much, much more important than that.***" I wouldn't perhaps go that far, but they're certainly far from being just a load of balls …

*Actually, rugby balls are not oval—they're prolate spheres (see page 32)

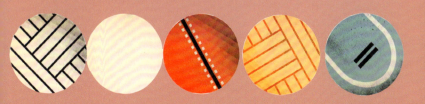

INTRODUCTION

1
BASKETBALL

> "I'm tired of hearing about money, money, money, money, money. I just want to play the game, drink Pepsi, wear Reebok."

SHAQUILLE O'NEAL
former NBA pro turned TV pundit

ODD BALLS

The smallest ever NBA (National Basketball Association) player was Muggsy Bogues at 5ft 3in (1.6m), who played for the Washington Bullets in the 1980s.

The tallest were Gheorghe Mureșan and Manute Bol, both at 7ft 7in (2.31m), who played for the Washington Bullets during the 1980s and 1990s.

Detroit Pistons' Isiah Thomas scored 16 points in 94 seconds against the New York Knicks in the 1984 NBA playoffs to force the game into overtime—and his team still lost.

The first professional basketball game was played in Toronto, Canada in 1946.

BASKETBALL

In 1992, two legendary MJs, Michaels Jackson and Jordan, appeared together in the music video for the King of Pop's single, *Jam.* A basketball that featured in the video was signed by the pair and, in 2010, was auctioned for a staggering $294,000. Jordan-related memorabilia is in high demand. In 1992, McDonalds released a limited-edition burger imaginatively titled the McJordan. A bottle of McJordan BBQ sauce was sold at auction for $9,995, 20 years later.

> Early basketballs were brown. Orange balls appeared in the 1950s and orange is still the official color for NBA balls. Other leagues use a variety of colors as well as multicolored basketballs.

Just two of the original NBA teams still exist today—the Boston Celtics and the New York Knicks. Every other original team has either folded or moved since the league started.

"Hockey is a sport for white men. Basketball is a sport for black men. Golf is a sport for white men dressed like black pimps."

TIGER WOODS professional golfer

> "If I weren't earning $3 million a year to dunk a basketball, most people on the street would run in the other direction if they saw me coming."

CHARLES BARKLEY
former NBA pro turned TV pundit

LEATHER FOR CHOICE

Early basketballs were made from four panels of leather stitched together with a rubber bladder inside. A cloth lining was added to the leather for support and uniformity, and, unlike modern balls, they had lacing. This was eventually abandoned in 1937, by which time basketball had become an Olympic sport, having been introduced the previous year in Berlin.

In 1970, the NBA adopted eight-panel rather than four-panel balls as the official ball, while in 1972, Spalding produced the first synthetic leather ball. But in 1983, the company's full-grain leather ball became the NBA's new official ball.

BASKETBALL

A PEACH OF AN IDEA

Despite being as American as apple pie, basketball was, in fact, invented by a Canadian, James Naismith, in 1891. Naismith was in charge of physical education at Springfield College, Massachusetts, and was looking for an indoor sport to play during the cold winter months.

Naismith's first version involved lobbing a soccer ball into an old peach basket. By 1893, peach baskets had been replaced by iron hoops and hammock-style baskets so that the referee didn't have to climb a ladder and remove the ball after every score.

The change to the basket wasn't the only amendment to Naismith's original rules. The first draft stated that there were nine players on each team and a "player cannot run with the ball" and "must throw it from the spot on which he catches it." In 2010, the first copy of the rules was bought by philanthropist David Booth for $4,338,500.

In 1894, at Naismith's behest, the first purpose-made basketballs were developed by the Spalding Sporting Goods Company. Spalding benefitted enormously from being there at the start, because when the official rules of the game were drawn up, they contained the phrase "… the ball made by A.G. Spalding & Bros. shall be the official ball."

BOUNCY, BOUNCY

In the nineties, basketballs with a textured pebble surface were introduced. These gave better contact between the players' finger pads and the ball, so that passing and shooting became more accurate, as well as making it easier to impart spin to the ball.

Today, a standard 29½in (75cm) basketball has about 4,118 "pebbles" on its outer surface, and the pebbles have a diameter of roughly a tenth of an inch (2.5mm).

Another major innovation came in 2001, when Spalding produced the Infusion ball, which had a built-in pump; and then in 2005 came the Never Flat, which the company guaranteed would have a consistent bounce for at least a year.

Not all innovations have been well received, however. In January 2006, the NBA introduced yet another new official ball, Spalding's Cross Traxxion, but players claimed that it was slippery, hard to hold, and the ball's increased friction cut their hands. In addition, the new ball bounced an average of 4in (10cm) less than the old leather ball. Unsurprisingly, it lasted just one season before the NBA went back to a traditional leather ball.

In 2021, the NBA dropped Spalding as its official game ball maker after more than 30 consecutive years. The NBA now uses Wilson, who had been the official ball provider between 1946 and 1983.

HE SHOOTS, HE SCORES

The record for the greatest height from which a basketball has been shot is 660ft 10in (201.4m). The feat, by YouTuber Derek Herron, was achieved in 2018 when he threw the ball from the top of Maletsunyane Falls in Lesotho, southern Africa, into a net positioned on the ground below.

Corey "Thunder" Law, a player from the Harlem Globetrotters, holds several world records for throwing a basketball into the hoop. In 2021, he broke the record for the farthest under the legs shot at 63ft 9.13in (19.4m). Then, in 2024, he made a record-breaking backward shot, nailing an 87-ft, 8-in (26.72-m) throw, as well as claiming the record for the farthest shot made while sitting on the court (70ft 6in/21.48m).

CURRENT BALLS

L eather remains one of the main materials of choice for the outer panels, although the molded rubber composite basketball was introduced in 1942. This had the advantages of being cheaper to produce and less prone to wear and tear, especially when used on rough outdoor surfaces.

Balls are generally designated for either indoor or all-surface use. Indoor-use balls are made of leather or absorbent composites and all-surface ones, known as indoor/outdoor balls, are made of rubber or durable composites.

Aside from Wilson and Spalding, another major basketball manufacturer is Molten, a Japanese company that has produced basketballs since 1958. Molten provides the International Basketball Federation (FIBA), the Olympic Games, and Super League Basketball with their official balls.

> Indoor balls are generally more expensive than all-surface ones, and may have to be broken in first to scuff up the surface for better grip when in play.

BASKETBALL

2
AMERICAN FOOTBALL

AMERICAN FOOTBALL

> "The word 'genius' isn't applicable in football. A genius is a guy like Norman Einstein."
>
> **JOE THEISMANN** sports analyst and former NFL quarterback

ODD BALLS

In the 1905 season, 19 players were killed and 150 seriously injured. President Theodore Roosevelt threatened to close the game down unless it was made safer.

According to declassified CIA records, Hitler's rallying cry "Sieg Heil!," meaning "Hail Victory," was modeled on the techniques used by American football cheerleaders.

Six new footballs, sealed in a special box and shipped by the manufacturer, are opened in the officials' locker room two hours and 45 minutes prior to the start of an NFL (National Football League) game. These balls are specially marked and used exclusively for kicking.

It takes about 3,000 cows to supply enough leather for a year's worth of footballs used by the NFL.

AMERICAN FOOTBALL

> If you applied for a Green Bay Packers' season ticket today, you might have to wait more than 60 years before receiving one.

Since 1941, the official supplier of balls to the NFL has been Wilson, the world's biggest manufacturer of American footballs.

Wilson produce some 2,500 balls per day, all by hand. Their Duke model has been used in every NFL game for more than 80 years.

According to a study in *The Wall Street Journal*, a standard NFL game on TV features just 10 minutes and 43 seconds of action, while commercials account for another 60 minutes or so of the three-hour game.

The average lifespan for an NFL player in 1994 was 55 years compared with 77.6 years for the rest of the US population.

AMERICAN FOOTBALL

During the 1958 NFL Championship game, a National Broadcasting Company (NBC) employee ran onto the field, posing as a fan, in order to delay the game, because the national TV feed went dead.

MOB RULE

In Jamestown, Virginia, "football" games in the early seventeenth century were similar to the various mob football games played in Britain, using a rudimentary ball made from an inflated pig's bladder.

In the early nineteenth century, students in universities such as Yale, Harvard, Princeton, and Dartmouth played with a ball similar to a British rugby ball. These games were spectacularly violent—so much so that Yale and Harvard banned them for a time in the 1860s.

In 1876, a set of rules was drawn up based on those of rugby union, and the Intercollegiate Football Association was formed. In the 1880s, Walter Camp, the "father of American football," introduced various new rules that differentiated the game from rugby.

GET A GRIP

B y the mid-nineteenth century, balls were being manufactured in a consistent shape, which made both kicking and handling easier.

In 1934, the circumference of the ball was set at its current size in order to make it easier to grip and throw, but other than improvements in the actual manufacturing process, the way an American football is made has changed relatively little in decades.

NFL football fields are often built facing north/south or in the shade, so that the sun doesn't interfere with play.

"You have to play this game like somebody just hit your mother with a two-by-four."

DAN BIRDWELL former NFL player

AMERICAN FOOTBALL

> "Most football players are temperamental. That's 90 percent temper and 10 percent mental."
>
> **DOUG PLANK** former NFL football coach

WHAT'S BROWN AND STICKY AND COMES FROM COWS?

The best American footballs are made from brown, tanned cowhide with various forms of weatherproofing and a "pebble grip" texture or tanning to provide a tacky grip.

The white stripes at either end of the ball are designed to improve grip. On top-quality balls they are stitched on rather than painted.

AMERICAN FOOTBALL

NFL players have been fined up to $5,000 for giving a game ball to a fan.

BALL CONSTRUCTION

In terms of construction, an American football consists of four panels that are stitched together, two of them being perforated along adjoining edges to allow for lacing. One of these two panels has an additional, reinforced perforation to hold the ball's inflation valve. An interior, multi-layer lining is attached to each panel to provide better shape and durability, and the panels are stitched together inside out, leaving the lacing hole, through which the panels are pushed after stitching to turn the ball right-side out. A three-ply polyurethane bladder is inserted through the lacing hole to improve air retention and moisture control.

The last process is inserting the laces, which are important for obtaining a good grip when holding and throwing, and may be made of leather or polyvinyl chloride (PVC).

HARDER, BETTER, FASTER, LONGER

The tackles regularly taken by American football players are some of the hardest in sport. A study by Virginia Tech revealed that players regularly receive hits of over 100Gs, sometimes reaching 150Gs—more than enough to knock the ball out of a player's hand. To give you a comparative force, a slap on the back is usually around 4Gs.

In 1940, the Chicago Bears beat the Washington Redskins 73–0, recording the biggest ever winning margin in an NFL game. The Redskins restored some pride 26 years later, when they defeated the New York Giants 72–41 in the highest-scoring NFL game of all time.

The fastest NFL player ever to take to the field game was Dallas Cowboys wide receiver, Robert "Bullet Bob" Hayes. Not only did he dominate on the football field but also on the track, where he won the 100 meters at the 1964 Summer Olympics, setting a new world record of 10.06 seconds in the process.

The longest successful field goal in an NFL game is by Justin Tucker of the Baltimore Ravens, who hoofed the ball 66 yards. In 2015, a video surfaced of a Texas Longhorns practice session, where kicker Nick Rose made an 80-yard field goal look easy.

3
VOLLEYBALL

ODD BALLS

The Beatles played a match on Sorrento Beach in Los Angeles in the early 1960s, watched by President John F. Kennedy.

Indian female beach volleyball players refused to wear bikinis in the 2008 World Beach Volleyball tournament.

The fastest recorded spike is 82 mph (132 km/h) by Bulgarian outside hitter Matey Kaziyski.

> "I used to go over to Gene Kelly's house and play volleyball, and Paul Newman and Marlon Brando were always there."

JOAN COLLINS actress and author

The longest recorded volleyball marathon is 101 hours and was achieved in 2017 by a student volleyball club in Amsterdam, Netherlands.

NO TOUCHING

Volleyball is derived from a game known as *mintonette*, which was invented on February 9, 1895 in Holyoke, Massachusetts by one William G. Morgan, a YMCA physical education director.

Most volleyball players jump about 300 times during a match.

Morgan wanted an alternative to basketball for older YMCA members, which involved less physical contact, so he took component parts of handball (hitting the ball) and tennis (the net) to make up his new game.

Sports ball manufacturer Spalding was contracted to make a ball for this new game, which became known as volleyball after the name was put forward by Alfred Halstead at an exhibition match in 1896.

Spalding's new ball had a rubber bladder and was the same size and weight as a modern volleyball. Indeed, there have been no changes to the dimensions since the earliest days of the game, and the design has remained much the same—typically, 18 rectangular panels of leather or synthetic material wrapped around a bladder, with a valve to regulate internal air pressure. The panels are arranged in six sections of three panels each.

BIGGER AND BRIGHTER

Beach volleyballs are slightly larger than regular volleyballs despite weighing the same, and have a rougher surface and a lower internal pressure, which makes them softer.

Generally, beach volleyballs tend to be more brightly colored than regular volleyballs. Those used to play the indoor game can come in a combination of colors as well as plain white.

IN GOOD COMPANY

Spalding's grip on the volleyball market was long ago broken by several other manufacturers, particularly those from Japan. In 1952, Tachikara produced a revolutionary seamless ball—referred to these days as a molded or laminated ball—in place of traditional asymmetrical hand-stitched balls. This improved the ball's shape, air retention, rebound, and overall durability.

Later developments by Tachikara include its patented Loose Bladder Construction (LBC) method, introduced in 1964, when volleyball made its debut at the Olympic Games in Tokyo. This allows a layer of air to circulate between the inside bladder and a cotton canvas/leather outside cover, resulting in a truer flight and a superior soft touch.

Tachikara's Dual Bladder Construction (DBC) volleyball appeared in 2003, featuring two internal, independent bladders. An impact-reducing layer of air circulates between the two, resulting in a ball that is theoretically twice as durable and responsive and has improved control and flight.

The official indoor and beach volleyballs of the Fédération Internationale de Volleyball (FIVB) are produced by Mikasa, a company with Japanese origins, now based in the USA.

Molten, also Japanese, have the top-of-the-range FLISTATEC. This is made from an outer layer of microfiber-based synthetic leather, which is as soft as natural leather and absorbs perspiration as well, but retains a dry surface better. Inside this is a rubber cover, which helps to improve durability and creates a better feel. This in turn contains a butyl bladder to prevent from air leaking out.

RUGBY

"I couldn't very well hit him, could I? I had the ball in my hands."

TOMMY BISHOP former rugby league player and coach, when questioned about kicking a fellow player

ODD BALLS

The first international rugby union match was between Scotland and England in 1871 at Raeburn Park in Edinburgh. Scotland won 1–0 after William Cross converted a try. Using the present-day scoring system, Scotland would have won 12–5 as they scored two tries and one conversion against England's one try, which they failed to convert.

Rugby Union featured in the Olympics in 1900, 1908, 1920, and 1924. The USA won on the last two occasions. Rugby sevens was introduced to the Olympics in 2016. Fiji won the men's gold medal in 2016 and 2020 but lost out to France in 2024.

Western Samoa's first international was against Fiji in 1924—there was a tree in the middle of the pitch and the game kicked off at 7 a.m. so the Samoans could go to work afterward.

> "Rugby is a game for the mentally deficient ... That is why it was invented by the British. Who else but an Englishman could invent an oval ball?"
>
> **PETER COOK** English comedian, actor, satirist, and writer

In 2007, an Australian rugby player complained of headaches and lethargy for some weeks after a game. A couple of months later, when he suffered a head injury that required examination, it was discovered he'd had another player's tooth embedded in his skull for all that time ...

The first national anthem sung at a rugby international was on November 16, 1905 when Wales played New Zealand at Cardiff Arms Park. After New Zealand performed the Haka (the Maori's ancestral war dance), the Welsh team responded with *Hen Wlad Fy Nhadau*, and the crowd joined in.

Morley RUFC (rugby union football club) remains a bastion of unionism in Yorkshire, northern England—the heartland of rugby league, as a result of the club's two representatives missing the 1895 meeting in Huddersfield, at which the split from union was organized. They decided to stop off for "a drink or two" *en route* to the meeting and consequently missed their train.

A try was so named because it gave the player who scored one the opportunity to try to score a goal by kicking the ball between two posts and over the crossbar, thus converting the try to a goal. The try itself actually earned no points at all.

The Gil Evans whistle is used to start the opening game of every Rugby Union World Cup. It was first used by Welsh referee Gil Evans in the match between England and New Zealand in 1905, and it was also used at the kick-off of the final of the 1924 Paris Olympics.

RUNNING WITH THE BALL

The invention of rugby is credited to William Webb Ellis of Rugby School in Warwickshire in 1823. A form of football in which the hands were used had been played at the school since 1750, but Webb Ellis took it further. He was accused of cheating, and consequently "held in low regard."

In the Roman game of *harpastum*, both hands and feet were used, and games such as "cnapan" in Pembrokeshire, Wales, "campball" in eastern England, "hurling to goales" in Cornwall, southwest England, and the "Atherstone Ball Game" in Warwickshire all date from medieval times and have similarities to modern-day rugby.

By 1845, Rugby School had developed rules for the game—prior to this, 300 or more players would take part in a school match—and the first balls made specifically for the sport were constructed in 1832 by William Gilbert (1799–1877). He was shoemaker to Rugby School and, in 1842, moved to premises directly opposite the school's playing field.

INFLATED BLADDERS

Early games used a bladder filled with paper or straw and no two balls were ever the same shape, size, or weight. Later balls were made from four pieces of cowhide stitched together and inflated by a pig's bladder, which gave the "prolate sphere" shape. The bladder, still green and smelly, was inflated through the stem of a clay pipe.

According to E.F.T. Bennett, who played for Rugby School in the mid-1800s, "The shape of our ball came from the bladder and was a perfect ball for long drop kicking or placing and for dribbling too …"

In 1870, Richard Lindop, a former pupil at Rugby School, invented an inflatable rubber bladder, which was both easier to blow up and helped prevent illnesses caused through inflating a raw pig's bladder by lung power.

> In the late nineteenth century, a ball inflator was invented, based on an enlarged ear syringe.

In 1871, William Gilbert's nephew James Gilbert exhibited the Rugby School Football at the Great Exhibition in London under "Educational Appliances" and went on to export rugby balls to British colonies, including Australia, New Zealand, and South Africa.

BALL INNOVATIONS

The Rugby Football Union (RFU) was founded in 1871, and in 1892 it introduced standard dimensions for the ball. Four panels became the official construction technique. Prior to this, six- and eight-panel balls were also produced.

Materials for the ball's outer covering included camel hide and pigskin as well as cowhide. The first two were easier to work with but were not popular with players since they were slippery when wet.

Henry Timms, who made some 50,000 balls for Gilbert between 1890 and 1935, introduced the technique of dry-leather stitching. Balls no longer had to be made up wet and dried out before being dispatched to market.

TWO CAN PLAY AT THAT GAME

In 1895, rugby split into two codes, union and league. This came about mainly as a result of the RFU enforcing amateurism on the game—a harsh imposition on the working-class northern clubs, whose players relied heavily on "broken-time payments" in order to take time off work to play the game.

There is very little difference between the balls used by union and league. Rugby League balls are a bit smaller and traditionally have six panels as this gives a more pointy shape, which is better for kicking, although today, four-panel balls are increasingly common. The balls may be similar but to quote sports historian Tony Collins, "The only thing the two sports really have in common is the shape of the posts and the balls."

NEW BALLS

The dimensions of the union ball were reduced by an inch (2.5cm) and the weight raised by 1.45oz (41g) in 1932 to make it better for handling, although different nations had their own design preferences. The Kiwis and Aussies preferred torpedo-shaped balls, South Africans went for eight panels for better grip, and the UK nations stayed with four panels.

Gilbert remained the main manufacturer for both union and league balls up to the 1970s. Gilbert Match, made from cowhide, was the standard issue for union internationals in 1960. For a while, Gilbert remained with natural leather as other companies moved on to various synthetics and laminates that reduced water retention and allowed better handling.

Companies such as Webb Ellis in England, and in rugby league, Steeden from Australia, are the other major players in the market today.

Gilbert still provides the official Rugby Union World Cup ball in the form of the iNNOVO match ball, which was used in the 2023 tournament and features patented dual valve technology for optimal balance and rotation, as well as defined, dual-height star-shaped pimples to aid grip.

In Australia, Steeden's name is often used generically for a rugby league ball.

A modern rugby ball is a complex composite of modern materials technology, using computational fluid dynamics analysis, nanotechnology, and 3D modeling to determine the optimum shape and placement of the pimples for minimum drag and maximum travel. All a far cry from a straw-filled bladder …

HIGH SCORES

The highest scoring game in the Rugby Union World Cup was when New Zealand beat Japan 145–17 on June 4, 1995.

The highest score in an international rugby league match is France's 120–0 defeat of Serbia and Montenegro in the Mediterranean Cup played in Beirut, Lebanon on October 22, 2003.

The highest score ever was recorded on February 8, 2015 in Belgium when Royal Kituro beat Soignies 356–3. Kituro ran in 56 tries, meaning they crossed the line roughly every 90 seconds.

5
TEN-PIN BOWLING

"There's kind of a Zen aspect to bowling. The pins are either staying up or down before you even throw your arm back."

JEFF BRIDGES actor and star of bowling movie *The Big Lebowski*

ODD BALLS

The largest bowling alley in the world is Inazawa Grand Bowl in Japan, with 116 lanes.

> The average speed of a bowling ball moving down the alley is 17–19 mph (27–31 km/h).

There are estimated to be over 100 million bowlers worldwide, making ten-pin bowling one of the world's most popular sports.

Henry VIII used cannonballs for bowling.

SCATTERING SKITTLES

The first game involving knocking down pins or skittles dates back more than 5,000 years to ancient Egypt.

The first written record of the game comes from 1366 when Edward III banned bowling in England as it was a distraction from training for warfare.

Meanwhile, in Germany, a game called *kegel* involved bowling at nine skittles. This, along with English and Dutch versions of bowling, was introduced to America during the colonial era. There is evidence of a ten-pin game being played in Britain in the early nineteenth century.

> Ten-pin bowling became popular in the USA after nine-pin bowling was banned in 1841, owing to its links with organized gambling. By this time, the first indoor bowling alley had opened in New York.

BALL TALK

The balls used in New York's first indoor bowling alley were made from a heavy wood known as *lignum vitae*, which is so dense that it will sink in water.

In 1905, the first rubber bowling ball was produced. In 1914, Brunswick began to manufacture Mineralite balls made from a hard rubber compound. Plastic balls were introduced in the 1970s.

In the early 1990s, Nu-Line developed the reactive resin surface, which is common on modern balls.

TEN-PIN BOWLING

6
FOOTBALL/ SOCCER

FOOTBALL/SOCCER

> "Some people believe football is a matter of life and death. I am very disappointed with that attitude ... It is much, much more important than that."
>
> **BILL SHANKLY**
> former professional player and manager of Liverpool FC

ODD BALLS

In 1979, a Scottish Cup tie between Falkirk and Inverness Thistle was postponed 29 times because of bad weather.

The Isles of Scilly have two football teams, the Gunners and the Wanderers. They play each other every week in the league, and also meet in cup ties.

The Albanian national team left the UK in disgrace in 1990 after a stopover at Heathrow, where they went on a literal free-for-all in the airport shops, believing that "duty free" meant "help yourself."

Pedro Gatica cycled from Argentina to Mexico for the 1986 World Cup, but couldn't afford to get into the matches, so he set about haggling for a ticket. While doing so, his bike was stolen.

Romanian midfielder Ion Radu was sold by second division Jiul Petrosani to Valcea in 1998 for 1,102lb (500kg) of pork.

FOOTBALL/SOCCER

DODGY DECISIONS

A Brazilian referee left the match where he'd been officiating on horseback at a swift gallop after shooting dead a player who disputed a penalty decision.

Danish referee Henning Erikstrup was officiating at the Norager versus Ebeltoft league match when, as he was about to blow for full-time, his dentures fell out. While he was searching for them, Ebeltoft leveled the score to 4–4, but despite their protests, Erikstrup disallowed the goal, popped his teeth back in, and blew the final whistle.

When the Football Association was set up in 1863, there was much discussion over Rule X: "… any player … shall be at liberty to charge, hold, trip or hack [his opponents]." It was subsequently dropped.

"A penalty is a cowardly way to score."

PELÉ
former professional player

FOOTBALL/SOCCER

> "I spent a lot of money on booze, birds, and fast cars. The rest I just squandered."

GEORGE BEST
former professional player

KEEP UP

In 2010, Dan Magness, a British football freestyler, kept a regulation football in the air for 26 hours using just his feet, legs, shoulders, and head. On another occasion, he managed to travel 36 miles (58km) while doing keepie-uppie, without letting the ball touch the ground, and in the process, visited five Premier League grounds in London.

In 1997, Milene Domingues (a former footballer, also the ex-wife of striker Ronaldo) broke the record for the longest keepie-uppie if measured by the number of touches accumulated—55,187.

FOOTBALL / SOCCER

"LOSER DIES"

In South America, 3,000 years ago, the Mayans played a form of football using a solid rubber ball weighing up to 20lb (9kg) and some 20in (51cm) in diameter. The losers were often sacrificed to the gods. The Aztecs played a similar "loser dies" game called *tlachtli*.

China's Han Dynasty (206 BC–220 AD) had a game called *tsu chu* (*tsu*, "kicking the ball with feet"; *chu*, "a stuffed ball made of leather") and the Japanese played a football-style game called *kemari* around 2,000 years ago.

In North America, Native Americans were recorded in the early seventeenth century playing a violent game of 500-a-side football called *pasuckuakohowog*.

The Aboriginal people of Australia's modern-day Victoria played a version of football called *marn grook*, while in the Middle Ages, Italy had *calcio* and France *soule* or *choule*, both using a stitched leather ball stuffed with leather and bran and deriving from a Roman game called *harpastum*.

FOOTBALL/SOCCER

HIDE YOUR CHILDREN

Football of sorts has been played in England from the eighth century onward. Games were played between neighboring towns and villages, involved hundreds of players, and often resulted in violence. The ball was an inflated pig's bladder encased in leather.

Modern-day examples of large-scale games can be seen in Christmas and Hogmanay events at Kirkwall in the Orkneys and Duns in Berwickshire, and Shrove Tuesday matches at Alnwick, Corfe Castle, and Sedgefield. Shop windows may be boarded up, and children and small dogs are ushered indoors to safety.

MAKING A BALL OF IT

In 1855, Charles Goodyear designed the first footballs to be made with vulcanized rubber bladders. Prior to this, balls made from pigs' bladders were standard.

The ball consisted of 18 sections arranged in six panels of three strips each, with a lace-up slit on one side. The ball case was stitched inside out and then reversed so the stitching was on the inside. A bladder was inserted and inflated through one remaining slit, which was then laced up.

The Football Association officially codified the rules of the game and, in 1872, decided on the weight and dimensions of the ball. To all intents and purposes, these are still in use today in world football.

During the early twentieth century, it was common for footballs to deflate during the course of a match.

The old brown leather balls would soak up moisture and gain considerable weight, and this, along with the protruding lacing, often resulted in head and neck injuries. As late as the 1970s, West Brom player Jeff Astle, and Danny Blanchflower of Spurs, both suffered chronic brain injuries as a result of heading heavy footballs, which eventually led to their deaths.

Later, various synthetics were applied to the ball's outer casing to repel water, and a new valve was introduced, which did away with the need to have a laced slit on the ball.

In the 1940s, a cloth carcass was inserted between the outer and the bladder to maintain the shape of the ball, as well as providing a certain amount of dampening and additional strength.

White balls were introduced in the 1950s as they were easier to see under floodlights, and orange balls were used in snowy conditions.

FOOTBALL/SOCCER

PANEL GAMES

In the 1950s, Danish company Select developed the 32-panel ball, which maintained a more spherical shape than the 18-panel version.

> **Black-and-white footballs were introduced for the 1970 Mexico World Cup, because they were easier to see on TV. The iconic Adidas Telstar ball had 12 black pentagons and 20 white hexagons.**

Numerous design improvements since then include the first fully synthetic football, the Adidas Tango Azteca in 1986, and in 2006, the Adidas Teamgeist, a high-tech, thermally bonded ball made up of 14 panels, used in the World Cup that year.

The latest development is the Nike Flight, which has a fuse-welded synthetic leather casing and a geometric four-panel design plus Aerowsculpt grooves, which, say Nike, are designed "to disrupt airflow across the ball for less drag and more stable flight."

All a far cry from a waterlogged leather lump that would deflate as the match progressed …

FOOTBALL/SOCCER

FOR THE LOVE OF THE GAME?

Much like their battle to be the world's best player, Cristiano Ronaldo and Lionel Messi also duke it out to be the world's highest earning footballer. According to *Forbes* magazine, Ronaldo topped the list in 2024, taking home a cool $285 million—that's over $32,500 every hour. Unlike in previous years, Messi took home less than half of Ronaldo's earnings, with a paycheck of $135 million.

At the opposite end of the pay scale is Kevin Poole. In 2013, English club Burton Albion suffered an injury crisis that left them without a reserve goalkeeper. Luckily, Poole, one of the club's coaches, was a former goalkeeper. He agreed to sit on the bench provided that Burton Albion paid him with cookies, specifically chocolate Hobnobs.

LONG-RANGE EFFORTS

The world record for the longest goal scored in a professional football match is held by Newport County goalkeeper Tom King. Playing against Cheltenham Town in January 2021, he hoofed the ball into the net from an incredible 105 yards (96.01m) away.

The fastest goal scored in a game is two seconds, when Nawaf Al Abed took a shot after being passed the ball from the kickoff. It was the first goal in a 4–0 victory for Al-Hilal against Al-Shoalah in the Saudi league.

FOOTBALL/SOCCER

RESPECT YOUR ELDERS

At the time of writing, the oldest active professional footballer is Kazuyoshi Miura, who at the age of 58 is a forward for Yokohama FC, a team from Japan's J-League.

The oldest player in English Football League history is Neil McBain, whose career spanned 33 years and seven clubs, including Manchester United and Liverpool. He retired in 1947 at the age of 51 but continued on in the game as a manager.

Older still is Israeli goalkeeper Isaak Hayik, the oldest player to participate in a professional game. In 2019, at the age of 73, Hayik played in goal for Israeli team Ironi Or Yehuda. He said he was "ready for another game" after playing for the full 90 minutes.

The youngest ever player in a professional match was Mauricio Baldivieso. In 2009, at the age of 12 years, 362 days, Baldivieso played as a striker for Bolivian side Aurora.

Scouting for young talent is a huge part of the modern game, but Belgian club FC Racing Boxberg took things to new extremes when they signed Bryce Brites, a 20-month-old baby.

FOOTBALL/SOCCER

7 TENNIS

"Tennis is a perfect combination of violent action taking place in an atmosphere of total tranquility."

BILLIE JEAN KING former world number one, founder of the Women's Tennis Association, World Team Tennis, and the Women's Sports Foundation

ODD BALLS

A tennis ball's coefficient of drag is calculated thus: Co = D/(0.5 q u^2 A) where D is the drag force, q is the density of air (1.21 kg/m^3), u is the velocity of the ball relative to the fluid, and A is the cross-sectional area.

The fuzzy surface of the felt is a vital component in how tennis balls travel through the air. It enables players to impart spin to the ball, since it creates air drag and friction, which allows backspin and topspin. Scientific papers have been written on the subject, and the ITF (International Tennis Federation) has tested tennis balls in wind tunnels and have a special rig designed to test ball spin with different rackets. Even NASA has studied the aerodynamics of tennis balls.

TENNIS

> "I love Wimbledon. But why don't they stage it in the summer?"
>
> **VIJAY AMRITRAJ** former tennis professional discussing the sodden 2007 Wimbledon Championships

Two possible origins of the word "tennis":

- From the French *tenez*, which means "take it/take that." This may have been shouted upon serving the ball in early games.
- From the game's possible—but very speculative—origins in Tinnis, an Egyptian town on the banks of the Nile.

The service was apparently invented by Henry VIII, who had servants throw the ball up for him to strike as he was unable to do it himself.

The longest match on record took place in 2010 at Wimbledon, when John Isner (USA) and Nicolas Mahut (France) played for 11 hours 5 minutes over three days in a game that Isner eventually won 6–4, 3–6, 6–7 (7), 7–6 (3), 70–68.

In the 1922 Wimbledon final, Suzanne Lenglen beat Molla Mallory in 23 minutes.

The use of "love" for zero is shrouded in mystery. One origin is said to be from the French word *l'oeuf*, as in "egg," meaning zero.

TENNIS

> The official world record speed for a tennis serve is held by Samuel Groth of Australia—163.4 mph (263 km/h) at the Busan Open 2012 Challenger Event. However, there is evidence (though often disputed) that Big Bill Tilden (USA) clocked up 163.6 mph (263.3 km/h) way back in 1931.

The tennis grounds at Wimbledon are owned by The All England Lawn Tennis Ground Plc and consist of 38 grass courts (18 for Championships, including Center Court and No.1 Court, and 20 for practice) as well as eight American Clay courts.

ECCLESIASTICAL TO REGAL PURSUIT

The first accounts of a game approximating to modern tennis originate in eleventh-century France, where monks knocked a crudely fashioned ball back and forth by hand over a rope stretched across a monastery quadrangle.

It was known as *jeu de paume*, due to the use of the palms. Around the twelfth century, leather gloves were introduced, then in the sixteenth century, short rackets—probably due to the fact that early tennis balls were made from leather stuffed with wool or horsehair and were hard on the palm of the hand.

By this time, the game had evolved into an indoor game, popular among French and British royalty and aristocracy, hence the term "court" for the playing area. This version of the game is still played and is known as Real or Court Tennis.

By the eighteenth century, the ball was made from thin strips of wool wound tightly around an inner core, which was then tied up with string. The whole lot was stitched inside a white cloth outer layer.

Major Walter Clopton Wingfield brought out two books on tennis, *The Book of the Game* (1873) and *The Major's Game of Lawn Tennis* (1874).

TENNIS MOVES OUTSIDE

Tennis, as we know it today, took off in Victorian times. In 1872, the world's first tennis club was formed in Leamington Spa, based on a game devised by Major Harry Gem and Augurio Pereira, while the following year, Major Walter Clopton Wingfield brought out a very similar game called *sphairistike* (from the Greek σφαίρίστική, meaning "skill at playing at ball") or lawn tennis. This was based on the old game played by royalty and used much of the French terminology of the original sport.

> "To be a tennis champion, you have to be inflexible. You have to be stubborn. You have to be arrogant. You have to be selfish and self-absorbed."

CHRIS EVERT former world number one and president of the Women's Tennis Association

At the first Wimbledon Championships, held in 1877, the balls consisted of solid India rubber spheres, although it was soon found that they lasted longer and were better to play with if flannel was stitched on top of the rubber.

The flannel was eventually replaced by hard-wearing Melton cloth, a tight-woven woollen cloth that originated in Melton Mowbray in Leicestershire, England. This felt fabric is still used today, along with Needle cloth, which is less hard-wearing.

According to the official Wimbledon website, 55,000 balls are used during the Championships. Balls are changed after the first seven games are played and then every nine games after that. Slazenger has been the official ball supplier to the Championships since 1902.

TENNIS

FEEL THE PRESSURE

Eventually, a hollow rubber sphere was introduced, which was cut to shape using "clover leaf" segments. The ball was filled with pressurizing gases, which were activated as the core was molded by heat into a spherical shape.

Later balls have two separate rubber hemispheres joined together under pressure to give a uniform shape and predictable response.

The felt fabric used on a modern tennis ball is woven using cotton and a wool/nylon mix, after which it's dyed and finished. Then two "dogbones" of fabric are cut, after application of a latex backing, and stuck to the latex-covered core. The ball is cured and tumbled slowly through a steam-laden atmosphere, which causes the cloth to fluff, giving a soft, raised surface. The ridge where the two halves of the ball are cemented together disappears.

The seam on a tennis ball is actually the glue that has come up through the two pieces of felt that make up the surface of the ball.

Logos are applied before the balls are packed in pressurized cans. Balls lose their pressure about a month after

TENNIS

opening the can. However, not all tennis balls are pressurized—you can buy pressureless balls with a solid core. These are used mainly for training. They don't lose their bounce like pressurized balls do, although the felt will wear off eventually.

PLENTY OF CHOICE

The ITF introduced yellow balls in 1972 (Wimbledon held off until 1986) because they are easier for TV viewers to see. Up until then, tennis balls were white, or occasionally black, depending on the background color of the court.

> Just one type of tennis ball was used in competition play until 1989 when high-altitude balls were introduced to allow for different atmospheric pressure. Then in 2002, Types 1, 2, and 3 balls became available—Type 1 for slower courts, 2 for standard courts, and 3 for fast courts.

Tennis balls vary slightly, depending on the manufacturer and model, and experienced players can instantly tell the difference between balls—they may feel lighter or heavier, harder or softer, more or less bouncy, have a coarser or finer cover, and require varying degrees of effort in order to generate the same speed.

TENNIS

8 PADEL

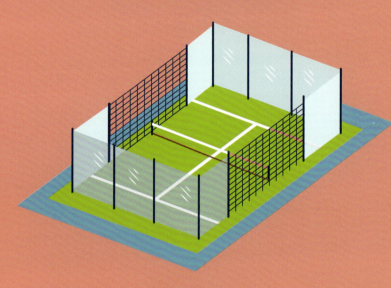

ODD BALLS

Padel is one of the world's fastest-growing sports, with more than 30 million players worldwide in 2024.

> "Although there is no official word to designate a padel player, there is nevertheless a certain consensus around the word 'padelista.' However, if you say 'padeleur,' you are not really wrong either."
>
> **FRANCK BINISTI** French padelista/padeleur

At the time of writing, there are two professional padel circuits—Premier Padel and A1 Padel. In the 2024 Premier Padel Circuit, there were stages in 18 countries on five continents.

Padel is derived from tennis, and the similarities between the two sports (and squash) are obvious. The sport is usually played in doubles on a court framed by glass and wire mesh and divided by a net, with players using a racket and a ball very similar to a tennis ball.

> The biggest difference between padel and tennis—and the biggest similarity to squash—is that balls can be played after bouncing off the walls.

PRINCE OF SPORTS

Unlike older sports, such as soccer, rugby, and cricket, the creation of padel can actually be traced to a single individual—the Mexican businessman Enrique Corcuera. Not having the space at his home in Acapulco, Mexico, to build a tennis court, in the 1960s, the savvy Signor Corcuera instead constructed a 66ft by 33ft (20m by 10m) court, framed by walls, and used it for a tennis-based game, which he called padel and played with a wooden bat.

> One of Corcuera's mates just happened to be Prince Alfonso Maximiliano Victorio Eugenio Alejandro María Pablo de la Santisima Trinidad y Todos los Santos de Hohenlohe-Langenburg (known to his pals, thankfully, as Prince Alfonso), who enjoyed the game so much that, in the 1970s, he took the idea back to his home in Spain.

Two padel courts were subsequently built in Marbella, and it wasn't long before the game spread throughout Spain (which is still one of its strongholds, along with Argentina), and the rest, as they say, is history.

ON THE BALL

It may look like a tennis ball, but a padel ball has a slightly smaller diameter of 2½–2⅔in (6.35–6.77cm), which results in subtle but significant differences in play behavior.

Padel balls also have a lower internal pressure than tennis balls (10–11 psi versus 14 psi), leading to lower ball speeds and less bounce. This results in longer rallies, and a game that followers claim generally requires more strategy and agility than tennis.

Padel balls are filled with gas, which means that, over time, they will slowly start to become softer, reducing their performance.

Among the major manufacturers of padel balls are Dunlop, Wilson, and Slazenger.

According to the International Padel Federation, padel balls should either be white or yellow.

PADEL

SQUASH

> "Squash—that's not exercise,
> it's flagellation."
>
> **NOËL COWARD** writer, actor, and singer,
> known for his wit and flamboyance

ODD BALLS

Early squash balls were a different size in the UK and the USA. One reason for this is said to be that a British squash official traveling to the USA with the "correct" dimensions for the ball happened to be aboard the *Titanic* and consequently never made it ...

The world-record speed for hitting a squash ball is 176 mph (283.25 km/h), which was achieved by Australian Cameron Pilley on May 9, 2014.

Squash is one of the best cardiovascular workouts you can get—in a one-hour game a decent player may burn between 700 and 1,000 calories.

The Avon India Rubber Company produced a squash ball in the 1920s that had a hole in it and was known as the Bath Club Holer.

SQUASHED BALL, NEW GAME

Squash began its journey to worldwide popularity at Harrow School, England, in the nineteenth century when pupils playing rackets and fives, both of which involve using a racket to whack a small hollow rubber ball against the sides of a four-walled-court, noticed that when the ball was punctured it allowed them to play a wider variety of shots.

Playing with a "squashed" ball took off, and squash soon became popular in other British public schools and universities, so that by 1908, a committee had been set up to organize the sport.

Up until the 1920s, there was wide variation in the size, weight, and composition of squash balls. They were universally made from rubber, but, for example, the Avon India Rubber Company produced balls varying from 1.5in (3.8cm) to 1.7in (4.3cm) in diameter with finishes that could be matt or varnished.

Squash balls were standardized in the 1920s, the Silvertown Company being a major manufacturer. After World War Two, Dunlop became the main supplier, followed by Slazenger in the sixties—they produced the first synthetic rubber ball.

In the early seventies, Dunlop introduced the colored dot on balls to mark their speed. Arguably the most popular, their balls are made from rubber mixed with combinations of different ingredients to produce the correct consistency for the particular speed of ball being made, which ranges from extra super slow (double yellow dot) to fast (blue dot).

S Q U A S H

10

TABLE TENNIS

> "Ping pong is coming home."
>
> **BORIS JOHNSON** the Mayor of London at the 2008 Beijing Olympics, during handover ceremony to London for the 2012 games

ODD BALLS

Table tennis was once banned in the Soviet Union because it was thought to be harmful to the eyes.

How many balls can two players hit back and forth in 60 seconds? The current record is 173, set by Jackie Bellinger and Lisa Lomas in 1993.

Table tennis paddles or bats are correctly known as rackets according to the International Table Tennis Federation (ITTF).

Official ITTF rules state that the ball should be white or orange. The choice of color of the ball might be made according to the table color and its surroundings.

Two players at the 1936 world championships in Prague took more than two hours to contest a single point.

ANYONE FOR TABLE TENNIS?

> Table tennis has also been known as ping pong, whiff waff, pom pom, netto, and tennis de salon.

The first table-tennis "balls" were made from the top of a Champagne cork or a rolled-up ball of string, in the 1880s. A line of books across a dining table made up the "net" and a cigar-box lid or book served as the "racket."

The first "Table Tennis" game was a board-and-dice game made in 1887 by J.H. Singer of New York and based on lawn tennis. In 1890, English company David Foster produced a miniature version of tennis as a table-top parlor game, featuring a 1in (2.5cm) cloth-covered rubber ball and strung rackets.

In 1898, London manufacturer John Jaques devised a new game called Gossima, which used rackets, a 2in (5cm) web-wrapped cork ball and a 12in (30cm) high net. This was renamed "Gossima or Ping-Pong" in 1900—the last part of the name was derived from the sound the ball made on the rackets.

Celluloid balls, which had just the right bounce, were introduced in 1900 to replace the rubber and cork balls. They were used until 2014 when, due to health concerns (celluloid is flammable), the ITTF decreed that the official material must be changed to plastic.

PICKLEBALL

ODD BALLS

Like padel, pickleball's origins can be traced with absolute certainty back to the 1960s—to the summer of 1965, to be precise. The game was invented in Washington state by Joel Pritchard and two of his friends, Barney McCallum and Bill Bell, to help keep their families entertained.

> "It felt like a big version of ping-pong."

ROGER FEDERER former professional tennis player

> The game can be played as either singles or doubles using smooth-surfaced rackets and a perforated, hollow plastic ball. Players volley the ball over a net, which is 34in (86cm) high—a bit lower than a tennis net.

Some tennis players may be disdainful of pickleball, but it has become especially popular in the USA, where it's now the fastest-growing sport, with around 20 million players in 2024 (and maybe as many as 48 million, depending on who's counting!), two professional tours, and two professional leagues. There are also professional leagues in Australia and India.

WHAT A PICKLE

So, what's the origin of the peculiar name of this sport? Well, coinventor Joel Pritchard's wife, Joan, explained: "The name of the game became pickle ball after I said it reminded me of the pickle boat in crew [rowing] where oarsmen were chosen from the leftovers of other boats."

> "To me, you'll see guys that didn't quite make it in tennis in college saying, 'Well, I'm going to turn to [pickleball].'"

JOHN MCENROE former professional tennis player

During the sport's creation, the three inventors improvised, initially making use of equipment from several other sports: a badminton court, table tennis rackets, a wiffle ball, and a net similar in height to a tennis net. (In case you're wondering what a wiffle ball is, it's a perforated plastic ball used in the sport of the same name—a kind of toned-down baseball.)

Pickleball now has its own standard ball, which, according to USA Pickleball (USAP), must be made of a durable material, molded with a smooth surface and have between 26 and 40 circular holes.

In 2022, pickleball was named the official state sport of Washington.

Typically, pickleballs for indoor use will have fewer, larger holes compared with outdoor balls.

> The ball must weigh 0.78–0.935oz (22.1–26.5g) and measure 2.87–2.97in (7.3–7.5cm) in diameter.

POPPING PICKLEBALLS

The sharp popping sound of a pickleball racket striking a ball can be loud enough to quite literally irritate the neighbors. In 2020, a park in Portland, Oregon, banned the game after local residents complained that they were unable to hold a conversation inside their homes such was the racket created by players whacking their pickleballs.

In August 2024, twin brothers Angelo and Ettore Rossetti set a world record for the longest pickleball volley rally, hitting 10,532 consecutive shots in 2 hours.

⑫ CRICKET

> "Cricket civilizes people and creates good gentlemen."

ROBERT MUGABE former President of Zimbabwe

ODD BALLS

The characteristics of a cricket ball change during the game. Fast bowlers prefer to play with a new ball since it is harder, travels faster, and bounces more than an older one. Older balls are better for spin bowlers because their rougher surface imparts better spin.

> Ball tampering can give bowlers an unfair advantage against batsmen. As a result, the rules of the game instruct that it's forbidden to:
>
> - Rub any substance apart from saliva or sweat onto the ball
> - Rub the ball on the ground
> - Scuff the ball with any rough object, including fingernails
> - Pick at or lift the seam of the ball

Rain stopping play is a common occurrence in cricket, but on rare occasions, the animal kingdom likes to throw a spanner in the works, too. In the past, a pig, sparrow, hedgehog, mouse, and a swarm of bees have all managed to halt progress on the pitch.

CRICKET

"Cricket is basically baseball on Valium."

ROBIN WILLIAMS actor and comedian

Shoaib Akhtar of Pakistan, also known as the "Rawalpindi Express," is regarded as the fastest bowler in the history of cricket. He set an official world record in 2003 with a delivery of 100.2 mph (161.3 km/h) against England in the World Cup.

How bowling speeds in cricket are classified:

	mph	km/h
Fast (express)	90+	145+
Fast-medium	80–89	129–145
Medium-fast	70–79	113–129
Medium	60–69	97–113
Medium-slow	50–59	80–97
Slow-medium	40–49	64–80
Slow	below 40	below 64

The Decision Review System (DRS) was introduced to cricket in 2008 and has revolutionized umpiring. This technology-based system uses various tools, including ultra-motion detection cameras and thermal imaging, to track balls. DRS helps the on-field umpires to make more informed decisions and to ensure fair play. Players can also utilize DRS if they wish to review or challenge a decision made by the umpire.

PUT A CORK IN IT

The essential ingredients of a modern cricket ball are very utilitarian—a core of cork layered with tightly wound string, which is then covered by a leather case.

Early cricket balls were even more basic. A lump of wood was used in an eighth-century Punjab bat-and-ball game called *gilli-danda*, and a game that involved throwing stones or sheep dung at an opponent, using a tree trunk or gate as a wicket, was played in south-east England shortly after the Norman invasion of 1066.

By the seventeenth century, things were more high-tech. Balls were made from leather stuffed with cloth, hair, and feathers, or a mix of cork and wool known as a "quilt." These were made by "quiltwinders" who wound a length of thread around an octagonal piece of cork to make a core for the leather-bound ball.

UNDER OR OVER ...

The first official regulations for the ball's dimensions date back to 1774, around the same time as underarm bowling began to be replaced by faster overarm bowling. The introduction of a standard size and weight for the ball helped both the batsmen and the bowlers since it made the delivery more predictable.

Edward "Lumpy" Stevens of Chertsey and, later, Surrey was one of the first bowlers to use the overarm delivery effectively.

A few years before this, the Duke family from the Eden Valley in Kent, England, started manufacturing the first six-seamed cricket ball, a forerunner of those used in the game today.

CRICKET

SQUEEZE AND SHINE

The cork core used in the balls gave bounce and hardness at the same time as providing enough give to ensure that wooden cricket bats were not damaged. The stitching around the ball was squashed down into a spherical shape with an instrument called, yes, a "squeezer." When the railways arrived, squeezers were often constructed from railway sleeper bolts.

Duke cricket balls are still in production today, and are said to keep their shine longer than other balls. The Duke Special County "A" Grade 1 red cricket ball is used exclusively for Test matches in the UK and first-class county cricket, while the Duke County International "A" is the choice of the majority of ECB (England and Wales Cricket Board) accredited Premier League games.

> "Down the mine I dreamed of cricket; I bowled imaginary balls in the dark; I sent the stumps spinning and heard them rattling in the tunnels."
>
> **HAROLD LARWOOD**
> Nottinghamshire and England fast bowler, and former coal miner

HIGH-TECH BALLS

Australian company Kookaburra was established in the late nineteenth century by English émigré Alfred Grace Thompson. Like all other successful cricket-ball manufacturers, Kookaburra moved from labor-intensive, hand-sewn balls to machine-manufactured products, opening a custom-built plant in Melbourne in 1946 and later developing state-of-the-art machines for cricket-ball production.

A similar path was followed in the UK by Alfred Reader & Company. Reader became one of the largest manufacturers of cricket balls in the UK, and by the 1970s was using high-tech research and development to produce balls made from synthetic cork. Reader worked in partnership with Tiflex Limited from Liskeard in Cornwall, which specializes in research into impact abrasion and vibration-absorbing compounds.

"You might not think that's cricket, and it's not, it's motor racing."

MURRAY WALKER motorsport commentator and journalist

> "... I have always looked upon cricket as organized loafing."

WILLIAM TEMPLE former Archbishop of Canterbury

RED OR WHITE?

The outside of a modern cricket ball is made from four separate pieces of leather. Two pairs are sewn together on the inside, forming two halves, and the join in one half is rotated at 90 degrees to the other. A raised seam between these two halves is sewn together with six rows of stitches made from string. The ball is then usually dyed red, but other colored balls, such as orange or yellow, are used for improved visibility, along with white for floodlit matches.

The origin of the traditional deep-red color of cricket balls is disputed, although one explanation is that it may have derived from the pigment reddle (red ocher), which was used to brand sheep.

Interestingly, white balls swing more and deteriorate faster than red balls—the polyurethane coating added to a white ball to prevent it getting dirty is the reason for the extra swing. Some people claim that white balls are harder than red ones, hurt fielders' hands, and can even break bats.

⓭ BASEBALL

> "Baseball, it is said, is only a game. True. And the Grand Canyon is only a hole in Arizona. Not all holes, or games, are created equal."
>
> **GEORGE WILL** US newspaper columnist

ODD BALLS

Before World War Two, baseball enjoyed some popularity in the UK. Many English football/soccer teams shared their grounds with baseball teams, which is why Derby County's former home was known as the Baseball Ground. In 1938, the Great Britain national team even managed to defeat the United States in the Amateur World Series.

John Smoltz, a pitcher for the Atlanta Braves, burned his chest in 1990 while ironing a shirt that he was wearing.

A curve ball can curve up to 17½in (44.5cm) in the course of being pitched, travels at between 70 and 80 mph (110 and 130 km/h), and rotates at 1900rpm.

All Major League Baseball (MLB) umpires must wear black underwear in case their pants split.

BASEBALL

Baseball is closely related to the old English game of rounders—at least according to an article written in 1905 by US sports journalist and Baseball Hall of Famer Henry Chadwick, although some aspects, such as the box score, are derived directly from cricket.

SPALDING'S CALL

From 1871 to 1875, A.G. Spalding, the "inventor" of the baseball as we know it today, pitched every game with a baseball he had developed himself. He won 241 out of 301 games, went on to be inducted in the Baseball Hall of Fame, and for the next 100 years, his baseball was the official ball of the US Major Leagues.

Over his career with Boston Red Stockings and Chicago White Stockings, Spalding achieved a 0.323 batting average, an earned-run average of 2.14, and an overall winning percentage of 0.796, a record that still stands today.

"I can wear a baseball cap; I am entitled to wear a baseball cap. I am genetically pre-disposed to wear a baseball cap, whereas most English people look wrong in a baseball cap."

BILL BRYSON author

"There are three types of baseball players: Those who make it happen, those who watch it happen, and those who wonder what happens."

TOMMY LASORDA former Major League player

MATERIAL THINGS

According to the official MLB rules, the ball "shall be a sphere formed by yarn wound around a small core of cork, rubber, or similar material, covered with two stripes of white horsehide or cowhide, tightly stitched together," a basic design that has changed remarkably little from the early baseballs invented by A.G. Spalding.

The MLB balls made today by Rawlings are still made from leather and have raised seams (with a regulation 108 stitches), a design that has been much the same for more than 90 years.

BASEBALL

"Half this game is 90 percent mental."

DANNY OZARK former Major League coach and manager

DEADBALL

Prior to 1872, when the dimensions and materials for baseballs were established, baseballs were made by hand from a string-wrapped rubber core with a horsehide cover, and varied from golf ball to softball size, and in weight from 3–6oz (85–170g). These early balls were renowned for their "deadball" feel in play, yet this was still a problem when the balls were standardized in 1872. This early period in baseball's history was known as the "Deadball Era" and home runs were a rarity due to the lack of response from the ball when whacked.

In 1910, George Reach of Reach Sporting Goods invented a baseball with a cork center, which was much more responsive. These balls were secretly used in the 1910 World Series (named after the *New York World* newspaper according to some; as a result of American hubris according to others) and with them, the number of home runs increased, leading to cork balls becoming the standard for Major League Baseball in 1911.

During World War Two, the US military developed the T-13 Beano hand grenade, which was designed to the same specifications as a baseball. The thinking behind this was that every American man should be familiar with throwing a baseball, therefore encouraging more accurate throwing by soldiers.

"Major League Baseball has asked its players to stop tossing baseballs into the stands during games, because they say fans fight over them and they get hurt. In fact, the Florida Marlins said that's why they never hit any home runs. It's a safety issue."

JAY LENO
comedian, writer, producer, and TV host

SMALL CHANGES

Pitchers developed new styles of deliveries to take full advantage of the more responsive ball. "Scuffballs," for instance, involved the pitcher rubbing a smooth spot on the ball, which caused it both to spin and travel more quickly. It's now banned due to the potential danger to the batter.

White balls became more common as they were easier for the batter to see and hit, which led to an increase in the number of runs being scored. To even things out, a 1931 change favored pitchers. A thin layer of rubber was wrapped around the cork core and the seams were raised. These changes deadened the ball slightly and the raised seams allowed pitchers to get a better grip to impart more rotation to the ball.

The number of balls used in a game from the 1920s onward could be between 20 and 60, because it became the fashion for fans to keep foul balls as souvenirs, instead of handing them in for free admission to another game. Also, umpires would remove dirty, worn, or scuffed balls from play much sooner than they had done previously.

- O - X - O - X - O - X - O -

> "Baseball is very big with my people. It figures. It's the only way we can get to shake a bat at a white man without starting a riot."

DICK GREGORY
African-American comedian, writer, and civil rights activist

No more noticeable changes took place in the design of the ball until Spalding, then the world's major manufacturer of baseballs and official supplier to the MLB, changed from cowhide to horsehide covers in 1974 for economic reasons.

> Today the average number of baseballs used per game is 120, with the average life span of a ball being five to seven pitches. The 30 MLB teams get through more than 900,000 balls each season, which costs somewhere in the order of a whopping $10 million per year.

> "If it wasn't for baseball, I'd be in either the penitentiary or the cemetery."

BABE RUTH former Major League player

BASEBALL

14

LACROSSE

> "I thought lacrosse was what you find in la church."

ROBIN WILLIAMS actor and comedian. No, it's not very funny but it's the only quote on lacrosse by a famous person

ODD BALLS

The word lacrosse is thought to be derived from the French term for field hockey, *"la jeu de la crosse."*

Lacrosse was a summer Olympic sport in 1904 and 1908—Canada won gold at both events.

A men's lacrosse team has 10 players—three attackers, three midfielders, three defenders, and a goalie.

The rules and field dimensions for women's lacrosse are different from men's. Each team has 12 players, usually four attackers, three midfielders, four defenders, and a goalie.

In the summer of 1763, two Native American tribes played lacrosse to distract British soldiers in order to recapture Fort Michilimackinac in Michigan.

ROLLING STONE

Lacrosse began as a game played by up to 1,000 men over three days, on a pitch as much as two miles (3km) long.

> At the end of a lacrosse game, the winning team gets to keep the ball.

> For Native Americans, lacrosse was a celebration of spiritual life and their environment. They played with a ball made from stone, clay, wood, knotted leather strips, or hair-stuffed deerskin.

European settlers took to the game and by 1867, lacrosse had been codified by the founder of Montreal Lacrosse Club, Dr William George Beers.

An indoor version of the game, box lacrosse, was introduced in the 1930s in Canada. Lacrosse is now Canada's official National Summer Sport.

GET A GRIP(PY)

Modern lacrosse balls are solid rubber spheres. They are usually white, orange, or yellow.

While most modern lacrosse balls are smooth, in 2002, Warrior Sports introduced the orange "grippy" ball to Major League Lacrosse to help fans follow the game both live and on TV. The grippy was textured, making it less weather-sensitive than other versions, and giving a better feel for the ball in the stick pocket.

> "If you are caught on a golf course during a storm and are afraid of lightning, hold up a 1-iron. Not even God can hit a 1-iron."

LEE TREVINO former professional golfer, who was struck by lightning while playing in the Western Open in Chicago in 1975

ODD BALLS

While playing a round in 1899, American Ab Smith produced what he described as a "bird of a shot," and the term "birdie" evolved from there.

The longest official recorded drive on an ordinary golf course is 515 yards by Michael Hoke Austin of Los Angeles, California, in the US National Seniors Open Championship in Las Vegas, Nevada on September 25, 1974.

A putt measured at 140ft 2¾in was sunk on the 18th hole at St Andrews by Bob Cook in the International Fourball Pro Am Tournament on October 1, 1976.

Pro golfer John Hudson scored two consecutive holes-in-one at the 11th and 12th holes (195 yards and 311 yards, respectively) in the 1971 Martini Tournament in Norwich, England. The chance of this is 67,000,000:1.

> The word "caddy" comes from the French "cadet," meaning "the boy" or "the youngest of the family."

Annual worldwide production of golf balls: 1.2 billion

The longest hole-in-one is thought to be 517 yards at the ninth hole of the Green Valley Ranch course, Denver, USA by Mike Crean in July 2002.

> "What most people don't understand is that UFOs are on a cosmic tourist route. That's why they're always seen in Arizona, Scotland, and New Mexico. Another thing to consider is that all three of those destinations are good places to play golf. So there's possibly some connection between aliens and golf."

ALICE COOPER
singer-songwriter whose brand of hard rock is designed to shock

CHANCES OF MAKING A SINGLE HOLE-IN-ONE?

- Professional golfer 2,500:1
- Average golfer 12,500:1

HAMMERS AND FEATHERS

The first golf balls were made from wood and were used in Scotland in 1550, although there are records of games similar to golf being played in China in the eleventh century and Holland in the thirteenth century.

A ball known as the "featherie" was introduced in Scotland in 1618, so called because it was made from a leather case packed with a "top hat full" of boiled goose or chicken feathers.

The materials were wet during construction so that as they dried out the feathers expanded and the leather contracted. The ball was hammered into a round shape, coated with several layers of paint, and punched with the ball maker's mark to create a hard ball that could be driven hundreds of yards.

80 percent of all golfers will never achieve a handicap of less than 18.

GOLF

The longest recorded drive of a featherie was 361 yards by Samuel Messieux in 1836 on St Andrews Old Course, Scotland, although a typical drive was 150–175 yards (compared with 180–250 yards with a modern ball).

Featheries were expensive, as were clubs, so golf was a rich man's sport.

PUT YOUR GUT INTO IT

In 1848, Rev. Dr Robert Adams Paterson of St Andrews introduced the "guttie" ball, which was less expensive than the featherie and could be repaired. It brought more people into the game.

The guttie was made by boiling *gutta-percha*, a rubbery tree sap, until it became soft and could be hand-rolled on a board into the correct size and shape.

A renowned maker of gutties was Allan Robertson of St Andrews, one of the first pro golfers. In 1859, he became the first person to record a round of under 80 on the Old Course at St Andrews.

Gutties with a rough surface were found to have a truer flight and travel farther than other versions, which led to balls being beaten with a sharp-edged hammer. By the 1880s, gutties were made in molds that created patterns on the surface—forerunners of the dimpled golf ball.

GOLF

> Rubber companies, such as Dunlop, began to mass-produce golf balls, which pretty much resulted in the end of hand-crafted balls.

HASKELL'S BALL

In 1898, US golfer Coburn Haskell came up with the next major development in golf balls, the rubber-core ball. Produced by rubber company B.F. Goodrich (later famous for their tires), these balls were made from a solid rubber core wrapped in rubber thread and encased in a gutta-percha outer casing. They gave the average golfer a good 20 yards extra length in driving from the tee.

In short order, the rubber-core golf ball went into mass production. In the early 1900s, gutta-percha balls were replaced with balata and in 1905, dimpled golf balls made their first appearance.

KING OF THE SWINGERS

The average speed of a PGA pro's swing is around 113 mph, which should send the ball a little under 300 yards. One of the game's biggest swingers is Bubba Watson. In 2015, his average swing speed was 123.5 mph and average drive distance was 315.2 yards. Compare this with one of the slowest swingers, Ben Crane, who had an average clubhead speed of 104.59 mph and drive distance of 271 yards.

DRAG ARTIST

Dimpled balls travel farther than smooth balls as a result of the turbulence caused by the dimples, which reduces drag.

The size and number of the dimples affects the ball's aerodynamics. There are no rules for how many dimples a ball can have—392 is the average and most have between 300 and 500.

Maximum permitted velocity of a golf ball: 250ft per second

The more dimples, the better the ball's stability in flight, but there's a trade-off. The more dimples, the less space between them, and if this is too narrow, it may shear on impact with either the club or the ground and the ball will scuff.

Most dimples ever on a golf ball: 1,070

A wide variation in ball sizes and weights existed when dimpled balls were introduced, and surprisingly it was not until 1991 that standard dimensions for golf balls were agreed between the two main golfing authorities, the Royal & Ancient in Scotland and the United States Golf Association in the USA.

GOLF

> "I have a tip that will take five strokes off anyone's golf game. It's called an eraser."
>
> **ARNOLD PALMER** former professional golfer

EXPLODING BALLS

B.F. Goodrich returned to the scene in 1906 with a pneumatic golf ball (known to explode in hot conditions), followed by experiments with cores of cork, mercury, and metal among other substances. However, the rubber-core golf ball remained the most popular until Spalding brought out the two-piece Executive ball in the 1970s.

Today there are essentially four different types of golf ball:

- One piece: basic, inexpensive balls made from a solid piece of Surlyn thermoplastic with molded dimples

- Two piece: hard-wearing balls suitable for long driving and popular with recreational golfers. Made with a solid, hard-plastic core of high-energy acrylate or resin covered with tough Surlyn or specialty plastic

- Three piece: made with a core that either contains a gel or liquid (such as sugar and water) or is solid, windings of rubber thread, and a plastic cover

- Four piece: made with a solid rubber core, two inner covers, and a thin but durable urethane outer layer to provide a longer hit and a better feel on the green

16
SOFTBALL

"If history repeats itself, I should think we can expect the same thing again."

TV COMMENTATOR Beijing Olympics softball competition, 2008

ODD BALLS

In October 2008, softball players in Kissimmee, Florida, had to rescue the pilot of a small plane who crashed after clipping the goalpost of a nearby football field on take off.

The official color for most softballs is yellow, although traditional white balls are also allowed, especially in the slow-pitch game.

Softball has also been known as kitten ball, diamond ball, cabbage ball, and pumpkin ball.

In Chicago it's common to play with an old-fashioned 16in (40.5cm) ball, which is softer than the standard 12in (30.5cm) ball and sometimes called a mush ball.

PLAYGROUND FUN

Disintegrating balls were an early problem in softball, so much so that sporting goods manufacturer A.G. Spalding were asked for help. They developed a ball smaller than an indoor baseball but bigger than a regular baseball. These "playground" balls were made with an elk hide cover. Raised seams protected the stitching from being worn away by the bat and the playing surface, and they were soft enough to be fielded without using a glove.

Walter Hakanson of the YMCA eventually came up with the official name "softball" at a 1926 meeting of the US National Recreation Congress. By 1934, the name was standardized throughout the country, as were the rules, and internationally the USA remains the number-one player of softball.

The ball has not changed much since the 1930s. Up to 2002, it was usually made up of two pieces of white leather or synthetic material in the shape of a figure of eight, sewn together with red thread. After that, the white leather was replaced by high-visibility yellow casings. The core may be made of long-fiber kapok, a mixture of cork and rubber, or a polyurethane mixture.

There are at least three different versions of how softball was invented …

- Thanksgiving Day 1887, Chicago, and alumni of Yale and Harvard universities begin knocking a boxing glove back and forth with a broom handle after an annual football match between them at the Farragut Boat Club. From this, two years later, George Hancock developed a proper bat and ball and the Farragut Club came up with rules for a game known as indoor baseball, using a 16in (40.5cm) diameter ball.

- A few years after this, firemen in Minneapolis were playing a similar game, kitten ball, invented by Lewis Rober Sr as an outdoor exercise for the fire crews. It used a 12in (30.5cm) diameter ball and had a different-sized diamond from the one used in Chicago (softball eventually combined the Minneapolis ball and the Chicago diamond).

- In 1916, employees of the Atchison, Topeka, and Santa Fe Railway in Kansas started to play a version of indoor baseball using a ball of only 5½–6in (14–15.25cm) diameter, which was so soft it was regularly smashed to pieces by the bat.

ACKNOWLEDGMENTS

The author would like to thank the team at Dog 'n' Bone for taking on this project.

The publisher would like to thank Blair Frame for his illustrations and Jerry Goldie for the design.

PICTURE CREDITS

Illustrations by Blair Frame, except for the following:
Stockgiu/Adobe Stock: p56
M. Usnata Wijaya/Adobe Stock: p57 & p59
skarin/Adobe Stock: p58
Teddy/Adobe Stock: p59
Ryantha/Adobe Stock: p64
DINVECT/Adobe Stock: p64
RATOCA/Adobe Stock: pp64–65
KayBeeSVGs/Adobe Stock: p65 & p67
D Graphics/Adobe Stock: pp66–67
JSalasberry/Adobe Stock: p67

ABOUT THE AUTHOR

Alf Alderson is an award-winning adventure sports and travel journalist and photographer based in Pembrokeshire, south-west Wales. His writing has appeared in a wide range of publications and websites including *Guardian*, *Daily Telegraph*, *Independent*, *Toronto Globe & Mail*, *South China Morning Post*, *Financial Times*, and *Mpora*. When he can be bothered, Alf posts scurrilous comments on his own blog, www.alfalderson.co.uk/blog. You can also find him on X: @alfinwales.